How to Play a Tune in Any Key

I0814670

by Collin Bay

1 2

Visit us on the Web at www.melbay.com — E-mail us at email@melbay.com

How to Play a Tune in Any Key

Being able to play a tune in any key is an integral skill for a musician to have. Perhaps you're a piano player accompanying a singer who either can't sing a particular song in a particular key due to a limited range, or who just wants to sing a song in a different key to give it a different color. Perhaps you're a jazz soloist and you've transcribed a soloist who plays a different instrument with a different range from yours; you may need to switch the key of the solo (or "transpose" the solo, to use the correct terminology) to be able to play it on your instrument. Or maybe you're part of an ensemble that just likes to change key, tempo, meter, and other elements of a song spontaneously for variety.

There's a very simple five-step trick to play any tune in any key. Many jazz musicians are aware of it, and some classical musicians regularly use it as well. To transpose a tune, one must learn its harmonic and melodic structure outside of the context of a specific key. Luckily the other elements of music are fixed: dynamics, rhythms, chord qualities, timbre, loudness and more, remain the same regardless of the chosen key for the performance of a song.

We'll use Red River Valley as a vehicle for learning the steps, but first a little theory.

Each key has a series of chords built on the various degrees of its scale. Take C major for example:

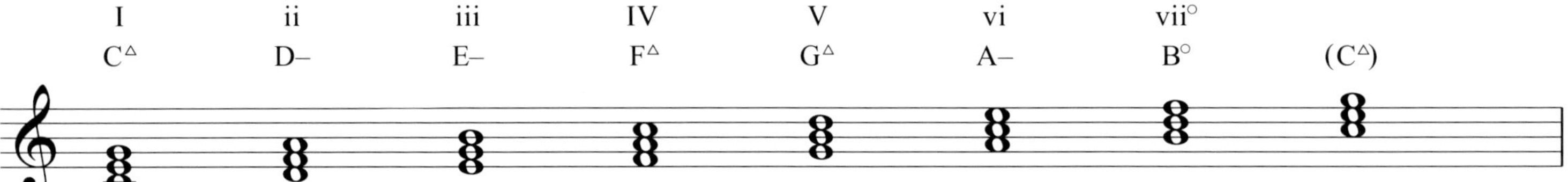

C is the first chord ("I"), the 'home' chord, or the "tonic". We give it an upper-case roman numeral because it's major.

D minor is the second chord ("ii"), written with a lower-case roman numeral because it's minor.
E minor is the third chord ("iii").
F major is the fourth ("IV").
G major is the fifth ("V").
A minor is the sixth ("vi").

B diminished is the seventh ("vii°"). We write it lower case even though it's a diminished triad because the third interval—b to d—is a minor third. It gets the circle to reflect the diminished triad.

Each of the roman numerals shows how the chord relates to the key of C; for example, F is the fourth chord and is major, so we label it "IV".

These relationships are true of every major scale. In other words, if we write out the chords from D major, they should each have the same relationship to the tonic (D), as they do in C major; so, the second chord will still be minor; the fourth chord, major; the seventh chord diminished, and so on:

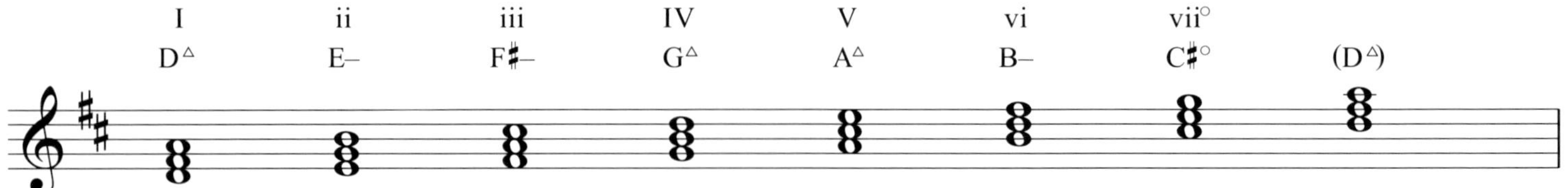

Even chords not found in the key of the piece have a relationship to the tonic. For example, an E♭7 isn't in the key of D but would be labeled ♭II7 (♭II because an E is the second of D, the root of the chord is an E♭ (or a flatted second), and II7 because the chord quality is a dominant seventh).

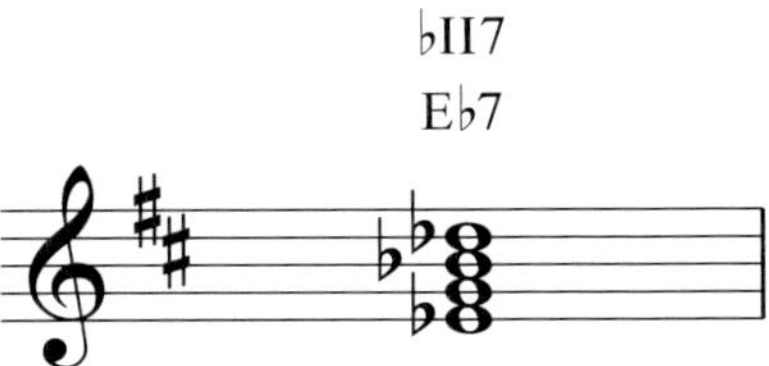

Some other examples:

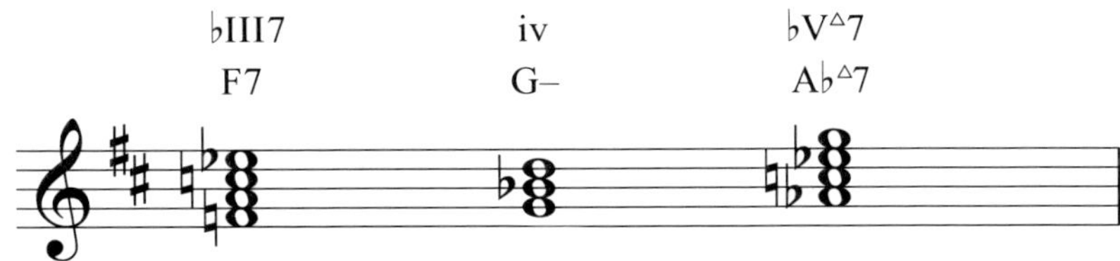

Red River Valley

Red River Valley is a simple tune. It's in the key of D major.

Red River Valley only makes use of three chords, all of which are diatonic to the key of D (they are, in other words, part of the D major family). The chords are D (I), A7 (V), and G (IV). Knowing that, we could label the chord symbols with their roman numerals:

Now chords aren't the only thing that have diatonic relationships; notes do too. As such, we can analyze the relationships the various melody notes in Red River Valley have to the chords in the song, and the key of the song.

There are two ways of analyzing melodies: you can either write out the relationship each note has to the key of the song, or you can write out how each note relates to the chord played behind it. For a simple, diatonic song like Red River Valley, going the former route is simpler and looks cleaner; however, when you get into more complex repertoire—music that changes key, or that has non-functional harmony—the latter method works better. As the latter method—showing a melody's numeric function in relation to the chord played behind it—is more useful, we'll go with it. Below you'll see Red River Valley's melody with the scale degree of each note:

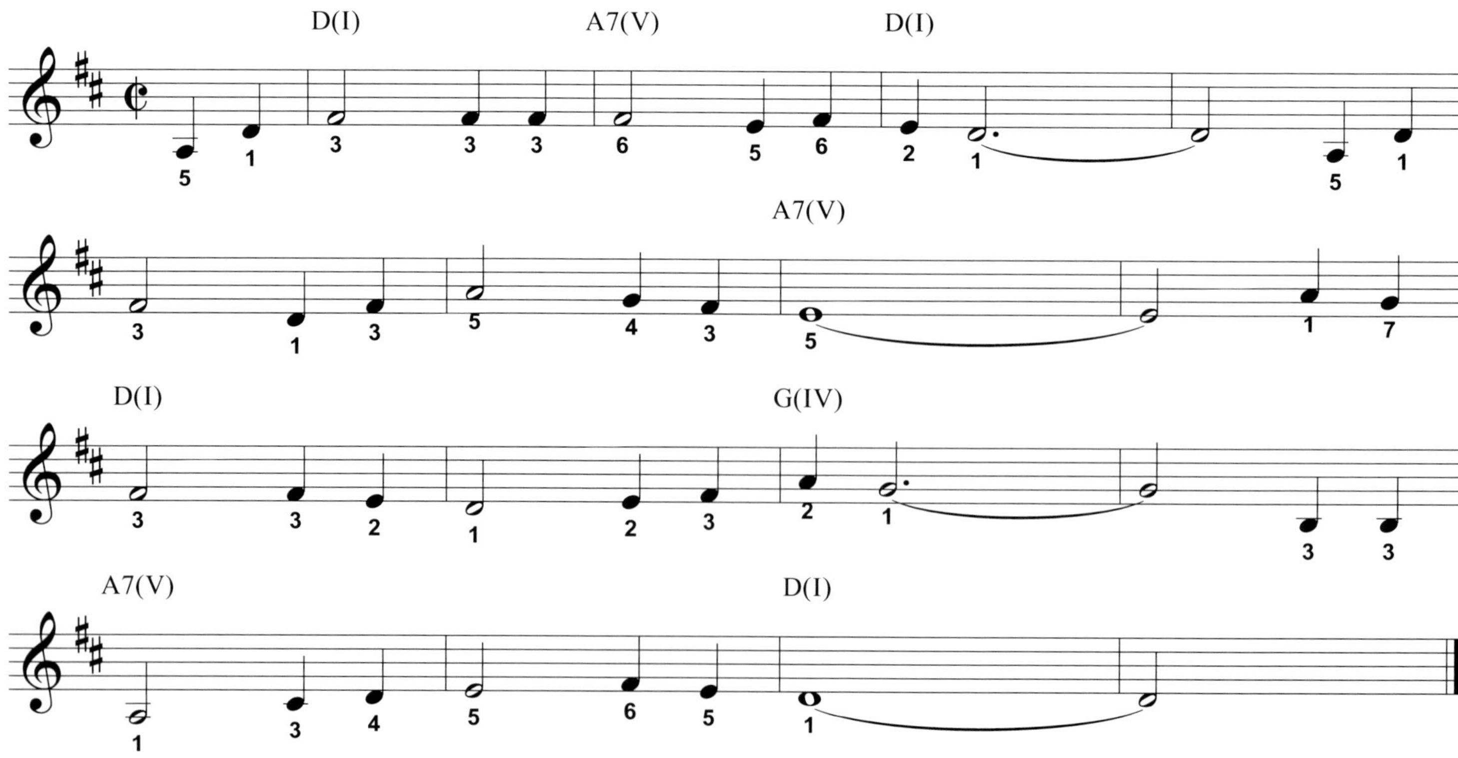

Now that we know the harmonic function of the chords and the scalar function of each melody note, we can easily translate Red River Valley into another key. Red River Valley is written below in C major:

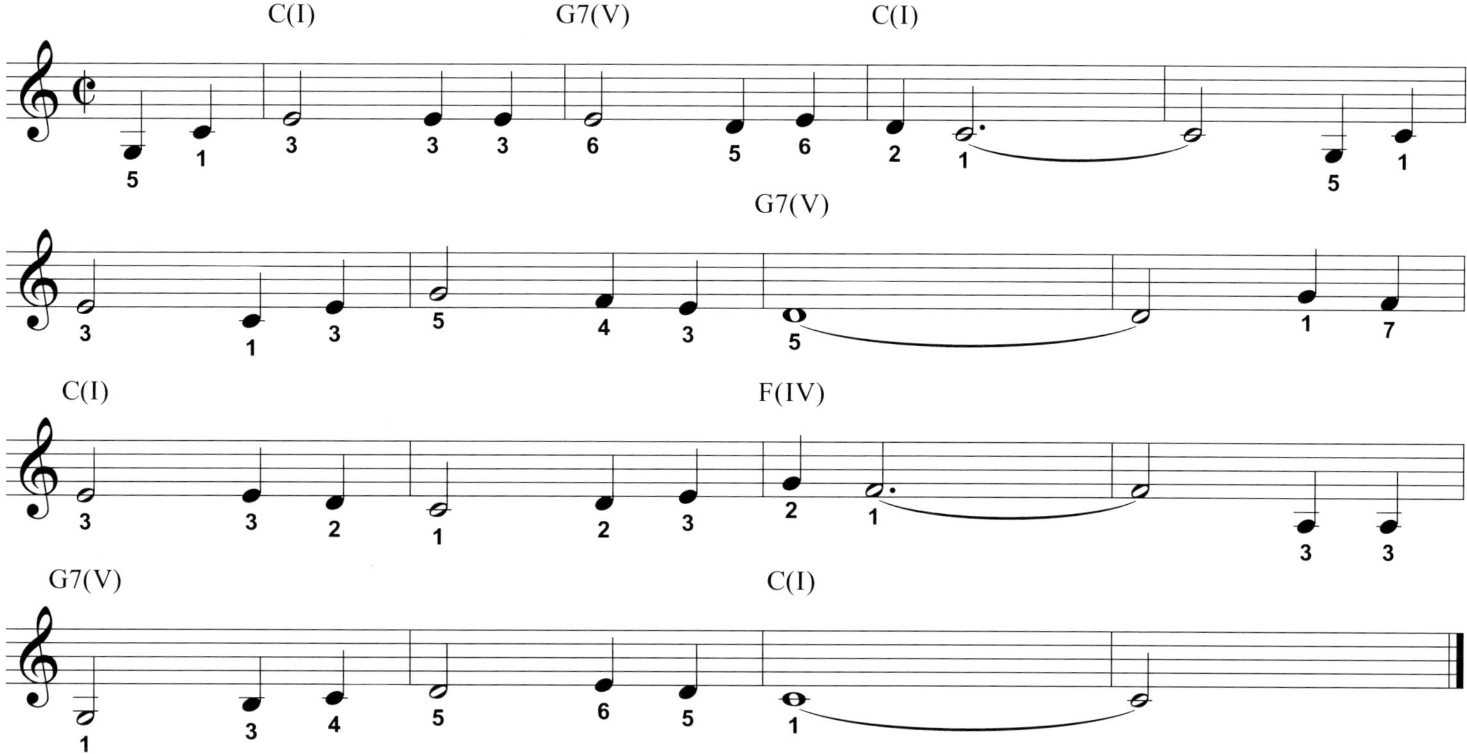

Let's review the steps:

I. Figure out the key of the piece and how each chord relates to it
II. Figure out how each melody note relates to the chord played behind it
III. Pick a new key to play the piece in
IV. Using the chord relationship represented by the roman numerals, fill in the chords for the new key
V. Using the scalar relationship of the melody, fill in the melody notes in the new key

This methodology works for pretty much every piece of music. There are several things to be aware of: first, not all pieces are composed in just one key. If you encounter a chord that doesn't relate diatonically to the key the music was written in, check to see whether or not the key signature changed on the staff – if so, you may need to use the new key to figure out the chord's function. Second, not all music uses functional harmony. Jazz musician Wayne Shorter, for example, often composed pieces in the 1960's featuring harmonically functional chords used in non-diatonic contexts. Those pieces can still be transposed – just make sure to maintain the chord quality and make note of the root movement (for example if the piece starts on C minor, then goes to G minor, then to B♭ minor, the root movement would start on C, descend by a perfect fourth, then ascend by a minor third):

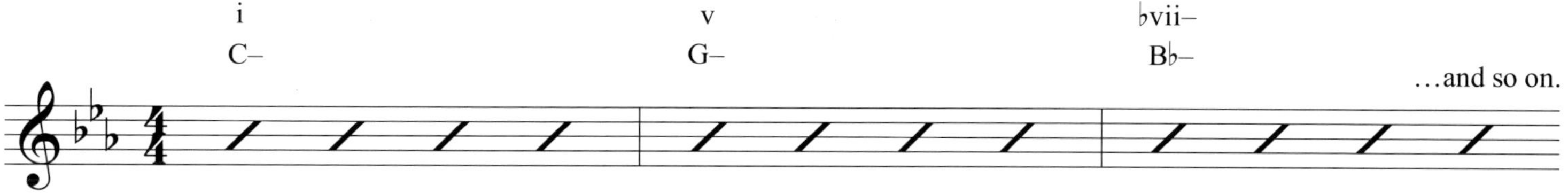

Transposed up a step:

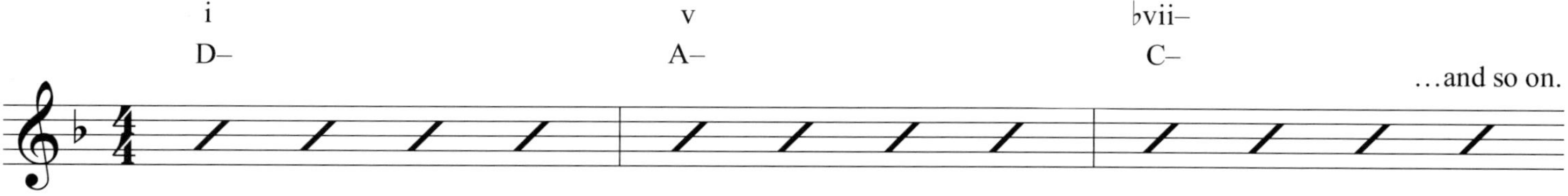

Just as chords exist in compositions that don't necessarily connect diatonically, melody notes also can exist outside of diatonic harmony. If you encounter a non-chord tone, you can still show how it relates to the chord behind it. For example, if the chord is a G7 and you encounter a melody line that consists of the notes B, C, C♯ and D, you could label them 3-4-4♯-5. Then you would transpose that using the same rules as before:

Transposed up a fifth:

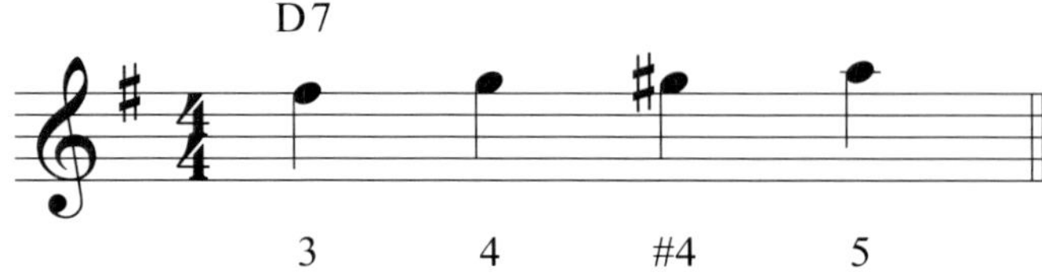

About the Author

Collin Bay began studying music as a four-year-old. He attended Interlochen Arts Academy and was part of the Interlochen Jazz Octet, recipient of Downbeat Magazine's top student award. He studied with Vijay Iyer and John Scofield at New School University in New York City. Fluent on many instruments and in many styles, he has performed on four continents both as a solo artist and as a member of various ensembles. He has shared the stage with MacArthur Fellows and has appeared on albums that have cracked the top-20 on iTunes world music chart. Having begun at Mel Bay editing books as a teen, Collin now works in Artist Relations and Product Development for the company. He resides in St. Louis and enjoys running with his dog. He is Mel Bay's youngest grandson.

MEL BAY